MUNRO LEAF

MANNERS CAN BE FUN

Third Edition

HarperTrophy

A Division of HarperCollinsPublishers

MANNERS CAN BE FUN
Copyright 1936, © 1958 by Munro Leaf, © 1985 by Margaret Leaf
Published in hardcover by HarperCollins Publishers.
All rights reserved.
Printed in Mexico.
Library of Congress Catalog Card Number: 84-48458
ISBN 0-397-32114-X
ISBN 0-06-443053-7 (pbk.)
First Harper Trophy edition, 1985.

Having good manners is really just
getting along well with other people.

If you lived all by yourself out on a
desert island, there would be no one to
care whether you had good manners
or not.

But if someone else lived on the island with you, you would have to learn to get along together. If you did not, you would probably argue and fight all the time, or—

stay apart and be lonesome because
you could not have a good time
together.

Neither would be much fun.

Most of us don't live alone on desert
islands.

So this is

what

we

do....

When We Meet People

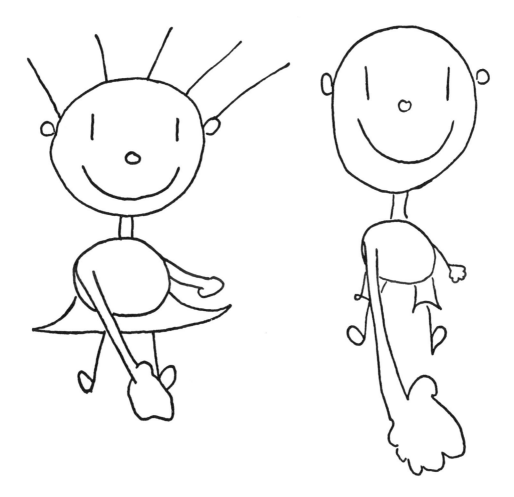

When I meet you for the first time I
smile and hold out my hand to you.

I don't just stand there with my mouth open and leave you holding out *your* hand.

If I already know you, I say

Good morning

or

Good afternoon

or

Good evening.

At Home

Very often the people we like most live in the same house with us.

We see them so often, we sometimes forget to be as nice to them as we are to others.

Most of the time it is just because we don't think of it, so let's see how we start the day.

We get up in the morning when we should,

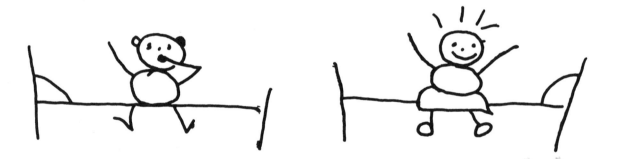

and we don't have to be called more than once.

We wash ourselves and brush our teeth without grumbling or making faces.

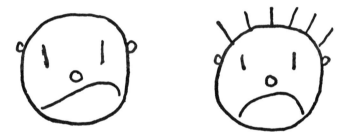

And we don't leave our clothes and towels around for others to pick up.

When we are at the table we enjoy
ourselves, because we eat what we

should and talk about things we have
seen and done.

We don't choke
because we don't talk
with our mouths full.

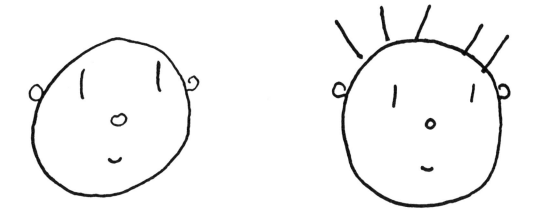

Other people like to talk to us because
we wait until they finish talking before
we start. We don't try to shout louder
and butt in like goats.

If we want something,
we say PLEASE.

We say THANK YOU if you help us or
give us something or do things for us.

Before we leave the table,

we ask if

we

may

be

excused.

And we say ☺ THANK YOU ☺
if we are told we may leave.

At Play

When we play with other children, we take turns doing the things we want to do. If we are playing games, we follow the rules. One of us doesn't always try to change things so that he or she will win. We play for fun.

We share our things and take turns
doing what we like most. We don't
whine and cry or quarrel when we
don't have everything our way,

and we don't
go home angry.

23

There are some people we don't like to play with, and here they are.

These are the PIGS.

They have all sorts of toys, but they
never let anyone else play with them.

They just squeal, THAT'S MINE.

This is a WHINY.

Whinies always cry because they can't do just what they want to.

They whine if they can't have things they should not.

They whine if they can't go along when they should not, and they whine when other people tell them No.

OH, HOW THEY WHINE.

These are the NOISIES.

They shout and scream and yell until I
can't even think. They make so much

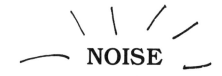

NOISE

they make me tired.

This is a ME FIRST
who never took turns.

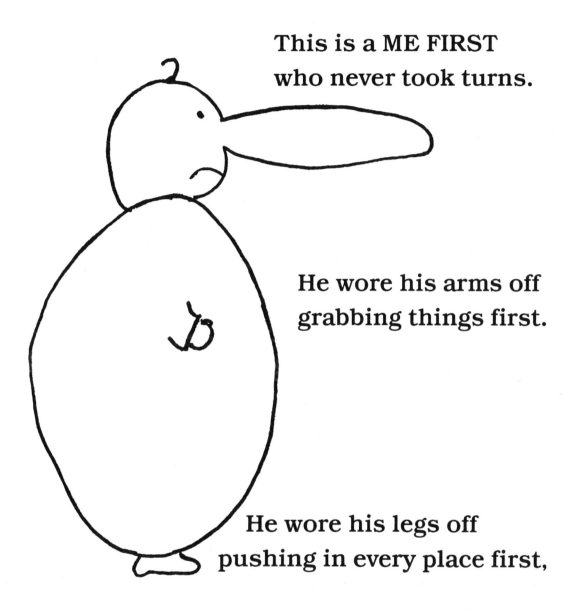

He wore his arms off
grabbing things first.

He wore his legs off
pushing in every place first,

and his nose is this way because he
was always poking it in to be first.

Here are SMASH, RIP, and RUIN.

SMASH is never happy unless
he is breaking things—
his things, your things,
everybody's things.

RIP is terrible. She destroys
everything she can tear.
Books, dresses, paper—
everything.

Sometimes RUIN uses a
hammer, sometimes ink
or paint, and sometimes
nothing but his hands.
But he always spoils
things so that no one can
enjoy them anymore.

SMASH, RIP, and RUIN

nearly always destroy

the things they use.

Or they forget to put them

back where they belong.

TOYS

Then other people

come along and step on them

or have to put things back for them.

When We Visit

When we go to visit someone,
we THANK them when we leave,
and we say GOOD-BYE.

Whether we are visiting or at home,
or at school or at play—

if other people like to do
things with us, it's probably
because

we

have

good

manners.

Just Plain Painful

Now let's have a look at some
creatures whose manners are just
plain painful. You can see why nobody
would want to have them around.

Here are two people so tiresome,

    it's hard to tell

        which is

            worse—

BRAGGER,
who tells you
all the time
how great he is
and how he can do
anything better
than anybody else,

and SHOW-OFF, who is
miserable if everybody
isn't paying attention
to her. Every minute
of every day she is
really saying the same
thing over and over—
"LOOK AT ME.
LOOK AT ME.
LOOK AT ME."

And here is
another one
who is no fun
to be with—

WON'T TRY.

Unless he knows
he can do something
best, he won't play
games or do anything
to help others have fun.

And slumped like a lump
in the corner is SULKY.

She can't have everything
her own way, so she is just
going to sit and sulk,
hoping to make everybody
else as unhappy as she is
making her silly self.

This little smudge
is a WON'T WASH.
The first lesson
in manners he needs is
what to do with soap,
water, a toothbrush,
and a comb.

And here goes a
BATHROOM WRECKER,
who makes a mess when he
does wash. He drops clothes,
washcloths, and towels anywhere.
He makes puddles on the floor,
leaves dirt rings in the tub and bowl
and hair in the brush and comb,
melts the soap, and has never
put the cap back on a
toothpaste tube.

How would you like to live with him?

SNOOPERS
walk right into rooms
where other people are
when the doors are closed.
If they knocked first and asked
if they might come in, people
would not call them
SNOOPERS.

This is TOUCHY.
Wherever he goes
he touches things.
He never thinks whether he
should or not.
Maybe it's because he
hasn't any head—
he is all hands.

And Touchy has a cousin named
GRABBER, who always takes the
biggest and the best piece of anything.

Some tiny babies don't know that they shouldn't suck their thumbs. But these creatures—

YAWNER   **SNEEZER**   **COUGHER**

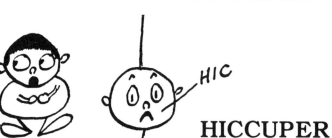

BURPER   **HICCUPER**

—are old enough to know they should cover their mouths and say EXCUSE ME!

Here you see a car full
of bad manners.

Old Grumpy with his arms folded and
that sour look is making everybody
unhappy. Ever since they started, he
has been whining, "When are we going
to get there?" and "How much farther
is it?" His trash-tossing sister is
trying to make our whole country as
messy as she is herself.

Some people don't know it, but there
are TELEVISION MANNERS too.

Pigging the best seat
and always saying
what shows to look at
is being crude and rude.
And if you don't stop
watching TV when you are told to—well,
that's not very good manners either.

See if you can't use a radio or record player
at the right time and place, so you don't
make other people unhappy with too
much NOISE.

When we are old enough to go to school, let's hope we are fair enough so we don't squawk and screech answers without taking turns or raising our hands.

Manners at school are mostly being FAIR.

When Night Comes

It is time for sleep, and people who like us all day long say GOOD NIGHT.

Then it is time for us to go.

Only WHINIES stand around saying,
"Do I have to go to sleep NOW?"

while we are first in...

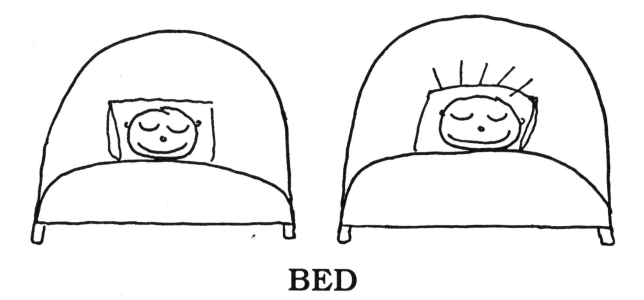

BED

Be kind to
ANIMALS.
They have feelings, too.